12 Tall Tale Mini-Books

by Jeannette Sanderson

Johnny Appleseed

Pecos Bill

Paul Bunyan

Davy Crockett

Febold Feboldson

John Henry

Mose Humphreys

Joe Magarac

Gib Morgan

Sam Patch

Slue-Foot Sue

Alfred Bulltop Stormalong

SCHOLASTIC
PROFESSIONAL BOOKS

New York ◻ Toronto ◻ London ◻ Auckland ◻ Sydney ◻ Mexico City ◻ New Delhi ◻ Hong Kong ◻ Buenos Aires

For Catie and Nolan—

I didn't lasso a cyclone,
or jump Niagara Falls;
I didn't plant an orchard,
or answer fire calls.

I didn't ride a catfish,
or sail the ocean blue;
instead I wrote this book,
which I dedicate to you.

Acknowledgment

I would also like to thank my editor,
Sarah Longhi, who worked especially hard
to make this the best book it could be.

Cover design by Kelli Thompson

Cover and interior illustrations by Margeaux Lucas

Interior design by Ellen Matlach Hassell
for Boultinghouse & Boultinghouse, Inc.

ISBN: 0-439-30963-8

Contents

Introduction

About This Book 4

About Tall Tales and Suggested Reading 5

Background and Teaching Activities 6

Mini-Books

Johnny Appleseed 11

Pecos Bill 17

Paul Bunyan 23

Davy Crockett 29

Febold Feboldson 35

John Henry 41

Mose Humphreys 47

Joe Magarac 53

Gib Morgan 59

Sam Patch 63

Slue-Foot Sue and Pecos Bill 69

Alfred Bulltop Stormalong 75

Introduction

About This Book

This collection of 12 mini-books will put some of America's best-known and best-loved tall tales into your children's hands, hearts, and memories. Easy to make and easy to read, these books will bring history and humor to all of your students, even those who are not confident readers. Written in a comic-book style, the illustrations, dialogue, and narrative text of each mini-book are inviting to readers of all levels and interests.

A brief overview of the tall tale genre and a list of books for further reading is on page 5.

Background information on each tall tale mini-book is included on pages 6–10. This section will include the following features for each mini-book:

Background This section gives the origin of each tall tale. It tells whether the tall tale is based on fact or is entirely fictional. It also includes any background information that might help students better understand the tall tale.

Vocabulary Potentially difficult or unfamiliar words in each mini-book are highlighted here. You might also consider pronouncing names and locations for students before they begin reading.

Teaching Activity An easy classroom activity for each mini-book is included to help reinforce the lesson.

How to Make the Mini-Books

1. Make double-sided photocopies of the mini-book pages. (Carefully tear along the perforation to remove the pages from the book.) Most mini-books consist of 6 letter-sized pages; only the Gib Morgan mini-book (pages 59–62) consists of 4.

   Note: If your machine does not have a double-sided function, first make copies of mini-book pages 1/3. Place these copies in the paper tray with the blank side facing up. Next, make a copy of mini-book pages 2/4 so that page 2 copies directly behind page 1 and page 4 copies directly behind page 3. Make a test copy to be sure the pages are positioned correctly. Repeat these steps with pages 5/7 and 6/8 and finally with 9/11 and 10/12.

   Regardless of how you make the double-sided copies, you may need to experiment to be sure the pages are aligned properly, and that page 2 appears directly behind page 1.

2. Cut apart the mini-book pages along the dashed line.

3. Place the pages in numerical order and then staple along the mini-book's spine.

4. Invite students to color the illustrations.

About Tall Tales

The dictionary defines a tall tale as a story that is exaggerated and difficult to believe. Most fans of tall tales would add that they're just plain fun!

Exaggerated storytelling has been around forever, though most of the tall tales retold in this book originated in America in the 1800s. They were born to satisfy two needs that people have always had but that were especially great in nineteenth-century America: the need for entertainment and the need for inspiration.

In the 1800s, people didn't have radios, televisions, and computers to provide entertainment to while away the hours between work and sleep. One of the most popular ways to spend a long evening was telling stories. Some of these stories started out as truth, some as pure fiction, but with many retellings most became taller and taller tales.

While entertaining, many of these tall tales also provided inspiration. The sailor setting out to sea, the pioneer setting out for distant lands, the freeman setting out to an unknown future—all these and more needed courage to help them face the challenges ahead. In *The Real Book of American Tall Tales*, Michael Gorham writes that tall tales "tell . . . that there's almost nothing a human being can't do if he sets his mind to it." These stories that showed what extraordinary people could do also hinted at what ordinary people might accomplish.

Most of these tall tales were first told orally and were later written down; some originated in print. We are lucky to have them today. Even in our fast-paced world with more entertainment options than the West once had trees, tall tales can entertain—and inspire.

Suggested Reading

For students:

Gorham, Michael. *The Real Book of American Tall Tales.* New York: Garden City Books, 1952.

Lisker, Tom. *Tall Tales: American Myths.* New York: Contemporary Perspectives, 1991.

Osborne, Mary Pope. *American Tall Tales.* New York: Knopf, 1991.

San Souci, Robert D. *Larger than Life: The Adventures of American Legendary Heroes.* New York: Doubleday, 1991.

Stoutenburg, Adrien. *American Tall Tales.* New York: Viking, 1966.

For teachers:

Blair, Walter. *Tall Tale America: A Legendary History of our Humorous Heroes.* New York: Coward, McCann & Geoghegan, 1944.

Botkin, B. A. *A Treasury of American Folklore.* New York: Crown, 1944.

Brown, Carolyn S. *The Tall Tale in American Folklore and Literature.* Knoxville: University of Tennessee Press, 1987.

Coffin, Tristram Potter, and Hennig Cohen. *The Parade of Heroes: Legendary Figures in American Lore.* New York: Doubleday, 1978.

Dorson, Richard M. *America in Legend: Folklore from the Colonial Period to the Present.* New York: Pantheon, 1973.

Dorson, Richard M. *Man and Beast in American Comic Legend.* Bloomington: Indiana University Press, 1982.

Haviland, Virginia. *North American Legends.* London: William Collins, 1979.

The Life Treasury of American Folklore. New York: Time, Inc., 1961.

Malcolmson, Anne. *Yankee Doodle's Cousins.* Boston: Houghton Mifflin, 1941.

Shay, Frank. *Here's Audacity.* New York: Macaulay, 1930.

Background and Teaching Activities

Johnny Appleseed

Background   This tall tale is based on the life of an actual person, John Chapman, an American pioneer who planted apple orchards in the wildernesses of Ohio, Indiana, and Illinois. Chapman was born in Massachusetts about 1775, moved to the Ohio River Valley as a young man, and for nearly 50 years traveled alone, planting apple orchards as the settlers moved westward. When he died in 1845, General Sam Houston spoke about him before Congress: "Farewell, dear old eccentric heart," he said. "Your labor has been a labor of love, and generations yet unborn will rise up and call you blessed."

While Chapman was a real person, many of the tales told about him are purely fictional. These tales began to be widely circulated after an 1871 article about him, "Johnny Appleseed, a Pioneer Hero," appeared in *Harper's New Monthly Magazine*.

Vocabulary
frontier: the far edge of a country, where few people live
mission: a special job or task

Activity   You can help students grow their own apple trees. Cut several apples in half crosswise, so that the stem is on one half. Take the seeds out of the apple core and put them in a cup of sand or dirt. Put the cup in the freezer for one month to trick the seeds into thinking it's winter. At the end of the month, take the seeds out of the cup and plant them in a flowerpot filled with soil. Place the pot in a sunny spot, water the seeds regularly, and watch them begin to sprout. When the seedlings are big enough, you can transplant them outdoors. Plant two near each other, as a lone apple tree won't bear fruit. Tell students to be patient, though: It takes many years for apples to grow on the trees.

Pecos Bill

Background   Pecos (pronounced PAY-kuhs or PAY-kohs) Bill is a purely fictitious character. The story of this legendary American cowboy started with a magazine article written by American journalist Edward O'Reilly in 1923 in *Century Magazine*. The author patterned Bill after Paul Bunyan, Davy Crockett, and other legendary heroes. While O'Reilly had Bill being raised by coyotes, riding an Oklahoma cyclone, and inventing many cowboy skills, the legend did not end with him. After the story was written, many others added their own twists to it. Pecos Bill has since become the subject of books, articles, poems, recordings, and plays.

Vocabulary
bleak: without hope
brand: to burn a mark on an animal's skin to show that the animal belongs to you
corral: a fenced area that holds horses, cattle, or other animals
cyclone: a storm with very strong, destructive winds that blow around a quiet center; a tornado
drought: a long spell of very dry weather
lasso: a length of rope with a large loop at one end that can be thrown over an animal to catch it
pasture: grazing land for animals
rope: to catch with a lasso or a rope
varmint: an undesirable animal

Activity   Ask students to make a baseball-like trading card for Pecos Bill, with his picture on one side and what they believe is the most important information about him on the other side.

Paul Bunyan

Background   No one knows how the legend of Paul Bunyan began, but the public first heard about this mythical lumberjack in 1910, when he was mentioned in a Detroit newspaper story by James MacGillivray. MacGillivray may have heard Paul Bunyan stories from lumberjacks, many of whom were French-Canadian and may have been embellishing French folktales of giants. When the Red River Lumber Company of Minneapolis began using Paul Bunyan in the company's advertising in 1914, the folk hero earned his place in American history. Since that time, Paul Bunyan has been the subject of stories, books, plays, and even ballets and operas.

To help students understand the context of this tall tale, tell them that the legend of Paul Bunyan began in the late nineteenth and early twentieth

centuries, when the United States was younger. At that time, forests covered most of the northern United States, from Maine to California. Lumberjacks cut down billions of trees to make lumber for houses, barns, churches, town halls, schools, bridges, wagons, and ships, among other things. They also cleared the land to make room for farms and villages. It was a time when little or no thought was given to conservation of forestland.

Vocabulary
bellow: to shout or roar
burlap: a tough, course material used to make bags that will hold heavy objects
hotcakes: pancakes
log: to cut down trees
lumberjack: someone whose job is to cut down trees and get the logs to a sawmill
sawmill: a place where people use machines to saw logs into lumber
timberland: wooded land

Activity   Ask students to choose a scene from the tall tale to illustrate as if for a newspaper of the day, and to write a caption to go with it.

Davy Crockett

Background   Davy Crockett, a real person, was born in the mountains of Tennessee in 1786. Like other frontiersmen of his day, Davy spent most of his time hunting, trapping, clearing land, and building home-steads. He was a U.S. Army scout and fought in the Creek Indian War. Davy became a local politician and eventually went on to serve several terms in the U.S. House of Representatives. When Davy lost his reelection bid in 1835, he decided to move to Texas for a fresh start. He died at the Alamo in 1836, fighting to help Texas win its independence from Mexico.

While Davy Crockett was real, most of the legends told about him are pure fiction. Davy was the originator of some of these tall tales. The man was an expert at a type of country exaggeration called "backwoods brag." One of his own tall tales was that a raccoon, aware of his skill with a gun, surrendered to Davy one day when the frontiersman was hunting. After Davy died, several books were published that told other exaggerated stories of the frontiersman's early life. These "Davy Crockett Almanacks" were just the beginning: In the nearly 200 years since his death,

Davy Crockett has been the subject of countless songs, books, plays, television shows, and movies.

Vocabulary
comet: a bright heavenly body with a long tail of light
crisis: a time of danger and difficulty
double-barreled shotgun: a shotgun that has two barrels, or tubes, from which bullets are discharged
frontiersman: someone who lives on the far edge of the country, where few others live
smithereens: bits, pieces

Activity   Tell students that Davy Crockett created some of his own tall tales when he engaged in "back-woods brag," a type of country exaggeration. Ask students to think of something they've done and exaggerate it into their own tall tales. Have students write, illustrate, and share their tall tales.

Febold Feboldson

Background   This tall tale of a giant Swedish pioneer in the Great Plains is based on a character whose name first appeared in print in 1923 in the Gothenburg, Nebraska, newspaper the *Independent*. Later stories about Febold were published in the *Gothenburg Times* from 1928 to 1933. The stories have been collected and retold many times since.

Where did Febold come from? Nebraska lumber dealer Wayne Carroll is credited with inventing Febold, though the tall tale character may be based on an actual Swedish pioneer of the 1800s. Real or not, Febold's tale echoes the stories of many actual pioneers, people who tried to make a life for themselves farming a land where drought, dust storms, grasshoppers, and extremes of hot and cold were all too common. These people had to learn new ways to do things to survive life on the Great Plains. Febold was the kind of hero who used his brain, and occasionally his brawn, to face down the elements.

Vocabulary
drought: a long spell of very dry weather
gizzards: innards
irrigation: system of supplying water to crops by artificial means, such as channels and pipes
vaporized: turned into fine particles of mist, steam, or smoke
varnished: given a clear coating to protect and finish; usually done on wood

Activity Divide the class into pairs. Ask each pair to write and then illustrate a two-page insert for the mini-book. The spread should show how the students imagine Febold Feboldson would have coped with another challenge—a dust storm, extreme hot or cold, or any other natural disaster—he might have faced on the Great Plains. Share these spreads with the class and compile them to make a sequel mini-book, *Further Adventures of Febold Feboldson*.

John Henry

Background According to some historians, this tall tale is based on an actual event involving an African-American steel driver named John Henry. The contest that culminates the tale is said to have taken place in the 1870s, during the excavation of Big Bend Tunnel for the Chesapeake & Ohio Railroad in West Virginia. The tunnel had to be blasted right through a mountain. This is how it was done: Steel drivers like John Henry hammered steel drills into the solid rock of the mountain. The holes made by these drills were then filled with explosives to blast away the rock for the tunnel.

According to a ballad based on the event, when a man brought a new steam drill to the site, claiming it could drill faster then a whole crew of men, John Henry stepped up and agreed to race the steam drill, to prove that man was mightier than machine. In the ballad, John Henry wins the race but dies of exhaustion.

After the actual event, the story took on a life of its own. Ballads, songs, and stories were written and sung about the man who first stood up to a machine. John Henry has been a hero to African Americans and all laborers ever since.

Vocabulary
steel driver: a man who uses a hammer to drill steel spikes into solid rock

Activity Tell students that just as John Henry did in the tall tale, most railroad workers sang work songs to help them get through the day. Most of these were short and repetitive, with pauses in between for the stroke of a pick or hammer. Ask students to write their own work song, either for a railroad worker or for themselves, to help them get through chores they have to do at school or at home. Encourage students to share these songs with their classmates.

Mose Humphreys

Background Mose Humphreys, America's first urban folk hero, was, fittingly, born on a Broadway stage. Mose was the hero of *A Glance at New York* by Benjamin A. Baker, which opened at the Olympic Theater in 1848. The star of the show, Mose, the "Bowery B'hoy," was based on an actual man, Moses Humphreys. Much like the character and legend he was to become, Moses was a printer on *The New York Sun*, a fire boy on the *Lady Washington No. 40,* and a notorious Bowery brawler.

The play was a huge success and other plays about Mose followed. The character even appeared in a ballet and in the circus! Mose Humphreys quickly became part of the popular culture. There were pamphlets, booklets, and posters about him. As one writer of the time wrote, "It is now impossible to write or talk of life in New York without a Mose."

Mose was a character of his time. He was a true "Bowery B'hoy," the term New Yorkers used to describe lively and playful men who hung out on the Bowery between 1846 and 1866. They were surly, talked in slang, and dressed extravagantly. They also did good deeds—keeping gangs in line and serving as the city's volunteer firefighters.

Vocabulary
muss: a fight
prospectors: people searching for gold
tenement: a run-down apartment building, especially one that is crowded and in a poor part of the city
trolley: a streetcar; a means of public transportation
wharf: a dock

Activity Discuss with students how Mose Humphreys was just one of many people who were, in some ways, replaced by machines. (You may want to discuss "John Henry" here also.) Ask students to brainstorm a list of jobs done by machines that were previously done by humans. Then ask each student to pick one machine and imagine they are the person who is being replaced by that machine. Have them write a diary entry telling that person's feelings about being replaced and what they plan to do next.

Joe Magarac

Background   Stories about Joe Magarac, the legendary hero of steelworkers, originated with Hungarian and other Eastern European immigrants who became steelworkers when they settled the steelmaking region of western Pennsylvania. The stories of this incredible man of steel have been passed down orally and have also appeared in print.

Vocabulary
boardinghouse: a lodging house where meals are provided
ladle: a large, deep spoon with a long handle
furnace: a large enclosed metal chamber in which fuel is burned to produce heat
molten: melted by heat

Activity   Ask students to bring in the obituary page(s) from a local newspaper, or provide it yourself, and have students read the longer, more detailed obituaries to see what kinds of information they provide. Then ask each student to write an obituary for Joe Magarac. You might want to ask students to illustrate a photo of Joe Magarac to include with the obituary.

Gib Morgan

Background   Gilbert Morgan was born on July 14, 1842, in Callensburg, Pennsylvania. Gib's family home was not far from Titusville, where the first oil well was drilled in 1859, when Gib was 17. After serving in the Civil War, Gib Morgan became an oilman, adopting the industry that had seemingly sprouted in his backyard. Like the oilmen of legend, the real Gib Morgan traveled all across the country drilling for oil.

The legend of Gib Morgan came from the man himself. Gib, whom his biographer called "the Münchhausen of the oil fields," was a storyteller as well as a driller. Gib made himself the larger-than-life hero in the numerous tales he told throughout his travels. Because he was such a good storyteller, his tales have survived more than a century, making Gib Morgan the tall tale hero more famous than Gib Morgan the man.

Vocabulary
cable: a thick wire or rope
cable drill: a cable with a heavy drilling tool called a *bit* on the end of it

derrick: a tall framework that holds the machines used to drill oil wells
divining rod: a forked stick that some people once believed could magically locate oil or water
dry hole: a well that doesn't have any oil
flapjacks: pancakes
prospect: to explore or search for something, such as oil or gold

Activity   Tell students that the real Gib Morgan was called "the Münchhausen of the oil fields." Explain that Baron Münchhausen was an eighteenth-century German hunter, soldier, and raconteur, or storyteller, who told exaggerated stories about himself in much the same way that Gib Morgan later did. Then ask students to think about something they've done in their lives that they can exaggerate into a tall tale. They may wish to make notes on this event. Then divide students into pairs and have them interview each other about the event. Ask the partners to write a brief—one- to two-page—summary of each other's exploits. Share these stories with the class.

Sam Patch

Background   According to most sources, Sam Patch, a real person, was born in Pawtucket, Rhode Island, in 1807. As a boy, he worked in a cotton mill just above Pawtucket Falls, where he took his first jumps. He later went to work at a cotton mill in Paterson, New Jersey. He made his jumps over the Passaic Falls during this time. These jumps made him famous, leading him to leave the cotton mills for a jumping career.

Sam Patch was invited to jump the Niagara Falls in the fall of 1829. He became a national hero after jumping there. One newspaper commented, "The jump of Patch is the greatest feat of the kind ever effected by man."

Not content to rest on his laurels, Sam Patch decided to build a twenty-five-foot scaffold on a rock overlooking Genesee Falls, in Rochester, New York, to prepare for his highest—125 feet—jump yet. Posters eerily announced *Higher Yet! Sam's Last Jump. . . . Some Things Can Be Done as Well as Others. There's No Mistake in Sam Patch.*

It was November 13, 1829. Sam made a short speech, then jumped. People later commented that he wasn't in his usual form, that he seemed to have been drinking. Whatever the reason, it was Sam Patch's final jump. He never reemerged, and his body was found four months later at the mouth of the Genesee River.

Even after his death, stories about Sam Patch lived on. Poems, ballads, rhymes, anecdotes, newspaper articles, tall tales, and plays celebrated this jumping hero. In many of the stories, Sam Patch's death was called a hoax. Some said he used a dummy for the final jump, or made the jump and hid on a shelving rock until the crowds dispersed. One story even said he jumped and came up on the other side of the earth!

Vocabulary

applause: approval shown by clapping hands

basin: a large bowl used for washing

festivities: activities that are part of a celebration

guide rope: a rope used to direct the placement of something

span: to reach over or stretch across

spectator: someone who watches an event but does not participate in it

Activity   Ask students to research some of the tallest places in the world. Then have each student make a poster advertising Sam Patch's leap from that place.

Slue-Foot Sue and Pecos Bill

Background   This tale is an adaptation of one of the many Pecos Bill (see above) stories.

Vocabulary

bareback: without a saddle

brand: to burn a mark on an animal's skin to show that the animal belongs to you

buck: when an animal jumps in the air with its head down and all four feet off the ground

buckskin: a strong, soft material made from the skin of a deer or sheep

bustle: a pad or frame worn by women in earlier times to puff out the back of a long skirt

courtship: attempts by one person to win the love of another

lariat: a lasso (see below)

lasso: a length of rope with a large loop at one end that can be thrown over an animal to catch it

rope: to catch with a lasso or a rope

shoe: to fit a shoe or shoes on a horse

slue: turned sideways

whirlwind: very quick and sudden

Activity   Ask students to write a poem that they think Pecos Bill might have written and given to Slue-Foot Sue before he asked her to marry him.

Alfred Bulltop Stormalong

Background   The legend of Alfred Bulltop Stormalong dates to the time of the great wooden clipper ships, which sailed the seas from the 1840s until the 1860s, when they were replaced by steamships. The giant sea captain of New England folklore made his first appearance in "Old Stormalong," a popular sea chantey sailors sang while they worked. This work song and other stories about Stormy emphasized his size and his adventures on the seas, especially on the *Courser*, the last ship on which he sailed.

Vocabulary

alter: to change something

bow: the front of a ship

cauldron: a large, rounded cooking pot

clipper: a fast sailing ship with three masts, built in the United States in the 1800s, and used to carry cargo

crow's nest: a small platform used for a lookout, found on top of the mast of a sailing ship

douse: to throw liquid on

fathom: a unit for measuring the depth of water; one fathom equals six feet

first mate: a ship's officer

hammock: a piece of strong cloth or net that is hung up by each end and used as a bed or a place to relax

mast: a tall pole that stands on the deck of a boat or ship and supports its sails

stern: the back end of a ship

unfurl: to unroll

weigh anchor: to pull up the anchor in preparation for sailing

Activity   Ask each student to choose an event in the story and to write an imaginary interview with Stormalong about that event. Then ask each student to write a newspaper article about the event, being sure to include portions of the interview with Stormy. Remind students to include a headline, byline, and dateline. You might also want to ask students to illustrate their articles. Share these newspaper stories with the class.

Johnny Appleseed

Two hundred years ago, Johnny Appleseed planted hundreds and hundreds of apple trees along the early frontier. You may have eaten one of his apples and not even known it. Why did he plant so many apple trees? He was on a mission. . . .

The only thing Johnny loved almost as much as apples was animals. And they loved him. He could cure them when they were sick, fix them when they were injured.

Here you go. And stop chasing those mice!

John Chapman was born in Leominster, Massachusetts, in 1775. The day he was born, a rainbow arched from one end of the sky to the apple tree outside his house. When Johnny saw the rainbow tree, he fell in love—with apples.

Johnny was a good baby, so long as you knew how to keep him happy. And it wasn't mother's milk or lullabies that made Johnny smile. It was a branch of apple blossoms.

Look at the beautiful rainbow! Look how it colors the apple blossoms!

Ga-ga ga-ga!

Don't cry now. Here are your apple blossoms.

As Johnny grew, so did his love for apples. When he realized that not everyone had apples to enjoy, it gave him something to think about.

I'd like to bring a sack of apples home to my family in the Ohio Territory.

Take them. And be sure to plant the seeds when you get home.

Johnny decided he would help the settlers by spreading apple trees all over the Midwest.

I am going to plant apple trees all over the new frontier.

What do you mean you have a mission?

Johnny gave thousands of apple seeds to others to plant. But he wanted to plant some, too. He abandoned his canoes and headed into the forest. He wore his cooking pot on his head and his sacks of seeds over his shoulder.

I will search for sunny places where I can plant apple orchards.

Johnny collected thousands of seeds. He dried them in the sun. Then he packed them into deerskin sacks, loaded them onto canoes, and paddled down the Ohio River. He gave apple seeds to settlers he saw along the way.

Whenever Johnny found a sunny clearing, he planted apple seeds. The forest animals would gather 'round to watch him. They were not afraid of him, nor he of them.

12 Tall Tale Mini-Books • Scholastic Professional Books

Johnny traveled across Ohio, Indiana, and Illinois. He was a strange sight with his cooking-pot hat, his old sugar-sack shirt, his bare feet. But settlers and Indians alike befriended him. They called him Johnny Appleseed. He planted apple seeds and he gave them away. He also helped in the orchards.

Johnny walked for years and years. He planted hundreds of apple trees. He gave away hundreds of seeds for people to plant their own apple trees.

Johnny usually slept outdoors. One bitter, cold night he wanted shelter. He started to crawl into a big, hollow log. A loud grunting and two big eyes told him it was already taken—by a bear! Johnny apologized, backed out of the log, and slept under the stars that night. Another night, Johnny heard a strange cry. He followed the sounds until he nearly tripped over a huge wolf. Its leg was caught in a steel trap. Johnny freed the wolf and bandaged its leg. The two became best friends.

Don't be afraid, brother wolf. I'll help you.

In 1845, Johnny Appleseed went to sleep in a barn in Indiana and never woke up. Some say his spirit still lives. Many of his apple trees do.

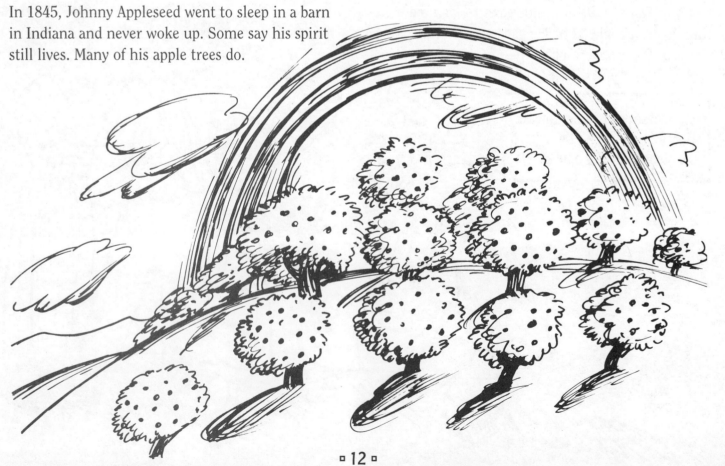

Pecos Bill

Cowboys wouldn't be cowboys if it weren't for Pecos Bill. It was about 150 years ago that Pecos Bill invented roping, branding, and all sorts of cowboy skills. Why, he even invented cowboy songs. Who was this cowboy of all cowboys?

When Bill was two years old, another family settled about 50 miles away. Bill's father decided the place was getting too crowded. So they packed up and headed west. When their wagon hit a big bump near the Pecos River, Bill bounced out. He hit the ground so hard the wind was knocked out of him. He tried to shout, but couldn't. With all those kids, his mother didn't notice him gone 'til the next day.

Our Bill is out there among the wild animals and rattlesnakes and such!

The varmints and wild animals will have to fend for themselves. Let's move on.

Pecos Bill was born in eastern Texas in the 1830s. Right away he stood out from his 17 brothers and sisters. He teethed on horseshoes instead of spoons. He drank the milk of a mountain lion instead of cow's milk. And he wrestled bears instead of brothers.

I'm worried about him!

OK, OK. Bill, you go easy on that bear!

Bill quickly found another family. He joined a pack of coyotes. They taught him everything they knew. He taught them everything he knew.

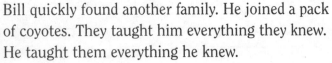

Keep practicin', you'll get it. Now, like me, A-woooooh!

A-wooooooh!

Bill grew up thinking he was a coyote. He might never have become a cowboy if Bowleg Gerber hadn't come along and set the ten-year-old straight.

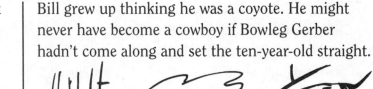

What do you mean, I'm not a coyote? I have fleas and can howl.

All Texans have fleas and can howl. But all coyotes have tails, which you don't have.

12 Tall Tale Mini-Books • Scholastic Professional Books

Once Bill realized he wasn't a coyote, he decided to become a cowboy like Bowleg Gerber. When Bill was a young man, Bowleg gave him directions to a cowboy camp down yonder a ways. Since Bill didn't have a horse, he rode a mountain lion instead. Bill followed Bowleg's directions to the cowboy camp. He was about halfway there when a 30-foot rattlesnake started shaking its tail at him.

Bill became a great cowboy. He and his men had a ranch so big that they used New Mexico as a corral and Arizona as a pasture. Bill invented all sorts of things to make being a cowboy easier and more fun.

Bill rode into the cowboy camp toward nightfall. He slid off his mountain lion and threw the rattlesnake, which he had been using as a whip, over his shoulder. The other cowboys stared at him with their mouths wide open.

Who's the boss around here?

I was. But from now on, I reckon you'll be.

12 Tall Tale Mini-Books • Scholastic Professional Books

One day Bill decided he wanted a horse. Not just any horse. He wanted the wildest, strongest, most beautiful horse he could find. It took a week to find him, a month to catch him, and nearly a year to break him! But Bill did break him.

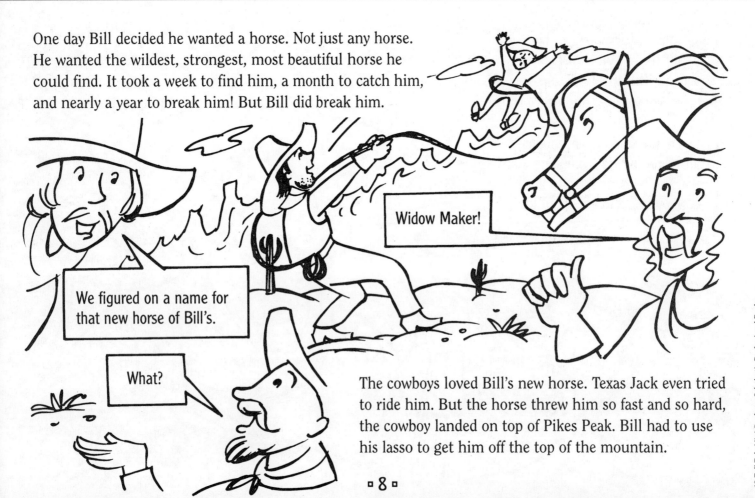

Widow Maker!

We figured on a name for that new horse of Bill's.

What?

The cowboys loved Bill's new horse. Texas Jack even tried to ride him. But the horse threw him so fast and so hard, the cowboy landed on top of Pikes Peak. Bill had to use his lasso to get him off the top of the mountain.

12 Tall Tale Mini-Books • Scholastic Professional Books

Bill and Widow Maker traveled all over the West rounding up cattle. Bill's ranch grew and grew. Then came the terrible drought. The grass dried up. The animals panted with thirst. The future looked bleak.

You got to do something, Bill.

This whole country's about to up and blow away.

Leave me think about it. I've never had to make rain before.

Bill roped that cyclone, pulled her down, and climbed onto her back. The cyclone twisted and turned like a wild bronco across four states, trying to throw Bill off. But Bill held on with his legs while he squeezed all the rain out of her.

Yippee! I'm makin' rain!

Bill rode all over the Southwest thinking about the problem. He kept looking for rain clouds. All he saw was clear sky until he reached Oklahoma. There he saw a big, whirling cyclone. The tornado frightened Widow Maker.

12 Tall Tale Mini-Books • Scholastic Professional Books

Bill let go of the rained-out cyclone in California. He fell so hard he made a giant hole in the ground. Today we call the place Death Valley. Bill didn't die there, though. It was a city man in a fancy cowboy suit that eventually killed Bill. Bill took one look at him, and he died laughing.

12 Tall Tale Mini-Books • Scholastic Professional Books

Paul Bunyan

Paul Bunyan was the greatest lumberjack who ever lived.
He was a giant of a man who cut down trees as easily as you
or I pick flowers. With the help of his great blue ox, Babe,
Paul Bunyan logged most of the United States.

Paul was so big that every time he rolled over in his sleep he would knock down trees, barns, even houses. Paul's folks were crazy about their new baby so they hardly noticed the trouble this caused. The neighbors weren't so forgiving. They told Paul's parents they had to do something about him.

Paul's father built a boat shaped like a cradle. He tied a rope to it and let Paul float out to sea. That seemed like a good solution until Paul got the hiccups. Then the boat rocked so hard it sent huge waves crashing toward shore. The people who weren't drowned hurried to Paul's folks.

Paul Bunyan was born in Maine, at least most of
him was. He was such a big baby, some people say
he was born in several states and part of Canada.

Canada

Vermont

New
Hampshire

Maine

Paul's parents took him deep into the woods of Maine. They found
a huge cave for him to live in. Paul's father gave him a giant cloth
sack. His mother gave him a giant sandwich and a kiss.

I'm sorry we have to do this, Son.
But everyone is safer this way.

Always remember you're Mama's
little boy and I love you.

Paul cried a river of tears when his folks left. When he stopped crying, he opened the burlap sack. In it was the biggest, shiniest ax he had ever seen. Paul picked up that ax and swung it. He easily cut down three trees!

This is fun! I'm going to be a lumberjack!

Paul and Babe became a team. They left Maine, which was too small for them, and headed out to Michigan. There Paul set up a logging camp on the Big Onion River, where he headed a group of mighty lumberjacks.

The main logging road in the north country was crazy crooked when Paul first got there. With all its twists and turns, it took hours to drive just a short distance. Paul straightened this problem out: He hitched Babe to the road and told him to pull until it was straight!

Pull, Babe! You can do it, I know you can!

Paul grew up to be the best lumberjack in Maine. He loved his work, but it was lonely having an ax as his only friend. Then, during the Winter of the Blue Snow, as Paul walked through the woods, he heard a bellowing from the frozen river. A baby ox had fallen through the ice! Paul sat on the riverbank and used his long arms to pull the ox out of the water. Paul noticed two things right away about the ox: It was as blue as the snow, and it was bigger than a full-grown bull!

You big, beautiful, blue babe! I'm going to take you home and care for you.

12 Tall Tale Mini-Books • Scholastic Professional Books

Paul even figured out a way to avoid having to carry trees to the sawmill. He hitched Babe to a square mile of timberland and had him pull it to the sawmill. Paul and his crew chopped down the trees right there. Then Babe dragged the cleared land back into place.

Let's bring that on down to the sawmill, Babe.

12 Tall Tale Mini-Books • Scholastic Professional Books

Paul also used Babe to fight forest fires. Whenever there was a fire, Paul would take Babe to the river for a long drink. Then Paul would tickle the animal in the ribs. Babe would laugh so hard, the water would squirt out of his nose and put out the fire.

□ 9 □

Once the Midwest was pretty well cleared, Paul and Babe headed west to find more work. As they passed through Arizona, Paul let his giant ax drag behind him. That's how the Grand Canyon was made.

□ 11 □

The men at Paul's camp worked up big appetites! Making enough hotcakes for so many loggers was no easy task. Paul got a dozen cement mixers to stir the batter. He built a griddle as big as a football field. And he hired 500 cooks to man the griddle. The loggers ate at mile-long tables. Men on bicycles rode down the center of these tables delivering the hotcakes while they were still hot. The bicycle riders had to be very careful not to skid on maple syrup and molasses!

Paul and Babe logged their way north through California and Canada until they eventually found themselves in Alaska. Today, if you happen to be in the great woods there, listen closely. You just might hear Paul's mighty cry.

Davy Crockett

Davy Crockett was the most famous frontiersman who ever lived. The great Tennessean could shoot sharper, run faster, jump higher, squat lower, dive deeper, and come out drier than any man in the whole country.

Davy's childhood revolved around animals. He loved to climb onto his sheepdog, Butcher, and chase bears that had just woken from their naps. You've never seen bears run so fast!

With all that fresh air and exercise, Davy grew fast. By the time he was eight years old, he weighed more than 100 pounds. He couldn't ride Butcher anymore, but he still liked to chase sleepy bears.

Davy Crockett was born in the mountains of Tennessee in 1786.
No one could agree if he was more like his mom or his dad.
Like his mom, Davy could leap over a seven-rail fence—backwards!
Like his dad, Davy could grin a hailstorm into sunshine.

12 Tall Tale Mini-Books • Scholastic Professional Books

Davy was so good with a gun he did most of the family's hunting. One day, he went down to the river to hunt with a double-barreled shotgun. He set his sights on a flock of geese in the sky and a big buck in the distance. Then he fired, sending a blast from each barrel. Davy hit the buck and the geese! The gun kicked so hard it knocked Davy into the river. Davy didn't mind: He came out dry, with his pockets full of fish. They were so heavy two coat buttons popped off. One killed a bear, the other a squirrel.

12 Tall Tale Mini-Books • Scholastic Professional Books

Davy was such a good shot that all the animals tried to stay clear of him. Once a raccoon saw Davy walk by with his favorite gun, Brown Bess, over his shoulder. The raccoon called down to Davy not to shoot, that he surrendered.

Don't shoot! I surrender!

Davy's grin proved as powerful as his gun. One day he saw a big raccoon sitting in a tree. As Davy aimed Brown Bess, he gave the animal his biggest grin. Didn't that raccoon fall dead right at Davy's feet, before Davy even took a shot at it!

That panther turned out to be a fine pet. Davy trained him to sweep the porch with its tail, rake the garden with its claws, and light his way to bed with its glowing eyes. The panther never killed again, though he was good at scaring away mice and strangers.

One night Davy was hunting and ran into the biggest, meanest panther this side of the Mississippi. Davy wanted to fight this fine animal fairly, so he dropped his gun, and the two began to wrestle. Before long, the panther was begging for his life.

Stop! Stop!

If you promise to stop killing, I'll bring you home with me. The young 'uns have been begging for a kitten.

12 Tall Tale Mini-Books • Scholastic Professional Books

Another day when Davy was out hunting he fell into an earthquake crack. A big brown bear pulled him free. Davy was so happy he hugged the bear. The bear hugged him back. Next thing you know, Davy had saddled the bear and was riding him like a horse.

Off we go, Death Hug! This should be an adventure! I heard some of them politicians are real animals!

Davy was so good at taming animals that his neighbors figured he'd be a good politician. They sent him to the U.S. House of Representatives in 1829. Davy was probably the first representative to ride "bearback" into Washington, D.C.

12 Tall Tale Mini-Books • Scholastic Professional Books

When Davy arrived in Washington, the country was in a crisis! A huge comet was headed for Earth. The president didn't know how to stop it from crashing into and destroying the United States. Then he saw Davy Crockett riding Death Hug down Pennsylvania Avenue.

One winter morning, back home in Tennessee, Davy was watching the sun rise over Daybreak Mountain. The sun got only a little way up and then froze. Davy hiked to the mountain's peak and saw that the sun had gotten jammed between two cakes of ice.

Davy rode Death Hug to the top of the tallest mountain. When the comet got close enough, Davy reached out and grabbed the comet's tail. Then he swung it around and around and let it go. That comet flew away from Earth faster than you can say, "Tennessee."

This'll teach you to bother Americans!

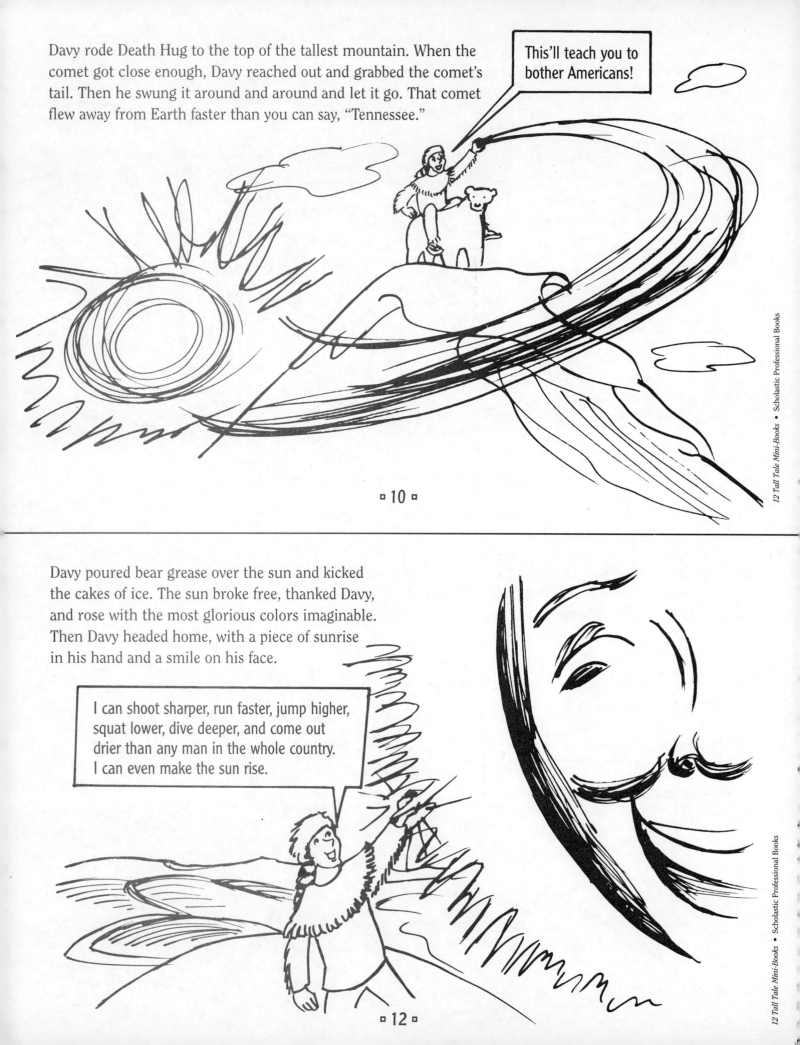

12 Tall Tale Mini-Books • Scholastic Professional Books

Davy poured bear grease over the sun and kicked the cakes of ice. The sun broke free, thanked Davy, and rose with the most glorious colors imaginable. Then Davy headed home, with a piece of sunrise in his hand and a smile on his face.

I can shoot sharper, run faster, jump higher, squat lower, dive deeper, and come out drier than any man in the whole country. I can even make the sun rise.

12 Tall Tale Mini-Books • Scholastic Professional Books

Febold Feboldson

Febold Feboldson was a giant of a man. But it was smarts rather than size that made this Swedish pioneer a hero of the Great Plains. Febold seemed able to outwit Mother Nature no matter what she threw at him.

□ 1 □

Then drought set in. There wasn't a drop of rain for weeks. The corn shriveled up and the cows about did the same. Febold had to tie weights to the cows' tails to keep them from blowing away. Febold's family began to think it had been a mistake to settle in Nebraska.

Febold Feboldson settled in Nebraska by accident. His family was halfway across America, on their way to California, when Grandfather took ill. While waiting for the old man to get well, Febold built a house, plowed a field, and planted a crop. In short, he made the Great Plains his home.

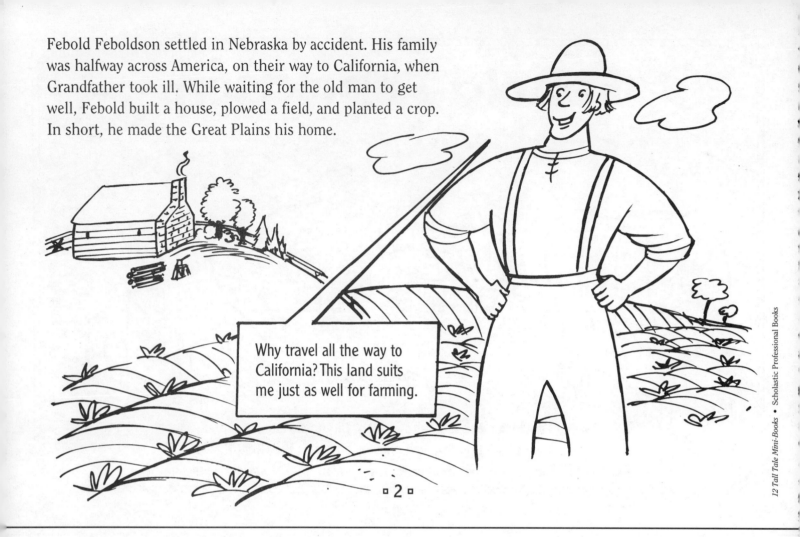

Why travel all the way to California? This land suits me just as well for farming.

12 Tall Tale Mini-Books • Scholastic Professional Books

Febold thought and thought about how to make rain. Then he lit on an idea. He built a big bonfire by the lake. The fire burned so hot that the water in the lake vaporized and turned into clouds. Once these clouds started crashing into each other, it began to pour.

Rain!

That's what you asked for, isn't it?

12 Tall Tale Mini-Books • Scholastic Professional Books

Febold's family didn't have long to celebrate the change in the weather. That's because the ground was so hot after the drought that none of the rain hit the ground. It just turned to steam. Soon the Great Plains was covered with the greatest fog the area has ever known.

Febold thought and thought about how to get rid of the fog. Then he lit on an idea. He parted the fog with his hands to find his way to the barn. Once there, he grabbed his giant pair of clippers and began slicing the fog into long strips.

When the turkeys arrived, the grasshoppers ate them, gizzards and all. Febold decided the only animals fierce enough to get rid of these grasshoppers were wolves. He went up to Canada and brought back several packs and, sure enough, they did the job.

After the rain and the fog, Febold's crops sprang back to life. They grew so big so fast that Febold became known as the best farmer in Nebraska. The next year his crops looked even better. He and his family were out in the fields admiring them when the sky turned black.

Did you make it rain again, Febold?

That's not rain, those are grasshoppers! What are we going to do?

Let me think on this. . . . I have it, I'll send back east for a flock of turkeys. Turkeys like to eat grasshoppers.

Febold thought and thought about how to get rid of the grasshoppers. It was hard to concentrate, because while he was thinking, the grasshoppers were munching away on Febold's beautiful crops. Finally, Febold lit on an idea.

▫6▫

Of course, since the grasshoppers had destroyed their crop, Febold's family didn't have much to eat, either. But Febold wasn't worried. He decided to go fishing. He brought Grandfather along with him.

How do you plan to catch fish without a rod or a net?

Easy. I'll just feed the fish raisins, which are loaded with iron. Then I'll use my magnet to pull them right out of the water.

▫8▫

12 Tall Tale Mini-Books • Scholastic Professional Books

The next year there was another drought, even worse than the first. Febold didn't want to make it rain again because the sides of the road were already pretty muddy from where he'd buried the fog last time. But he had to do something.

Febold did more than take care of droughts, fog, and grasshoppers. Why, he even caught a few cyclones and sent them back where they came from. Febold did such a good job outwitting Mother Nature that more and more people came to live on the Great Plains. Now that they had neighbors, they needed fences. But there was no wood or stones to build with. Febold set to thinking again. Febold thought and thought. Then he lit on an idea. He dug a bunch of holes in the ground, filled them with water, and let them freeze all winter. He dug the ice poles up in the spring and varnished them. Then he put them partway back in the ground and strung them with barbed wire.

Febold thought and thought. Then he lit on an idea. He would have to invent irrigation. He went all the way to the Platte River and, with the help of his pet buffalo, dragged the river back to his farm. Then he spread the water over his land through little ditches.

You did it again, Febold!

We'll have the tallest corn in Nebraska!

I just don't know why I didn't invent irrigation sooner.

Febold's wife sent a letter to a friend in California telling her all the great things Febold had done in the Great Plains. This friend wrote back asking if Febold could come to California and help the people there get rid of droughts and earthquakes. Febold and his family decided to go.

Have you figured out how to stop earthquakes?

I'm thinking on it.

When Febold arrived in California, he went straight to work. He made rain and taught Californians his irrigation invention. The earthquake problem is taking a little longer to figure out. People there are pretty confident, though: If anyone can figure a way to tame Mother Nature, it's Febold Feboldson.

John Henry

Imagine a contest between a man and a machine, a contest between a strong, powerful steel driver and a brand-new steam-powered drill. Would the man or the machine win? That depends on the man. If it was John Henry, well . . .

John Henry was an easy baby. All he needed to keep happy was a pile of food to eat and a pile of rocks to hammer. Johnny wasn't two years old when he was hammering rocks into powder finer than cornmeal!

Will you look at him eat!

Will you look at him hammer! He's going to be a steel-driving man!

The night John Henry was born, lightning lit the sky and thunder hammered the air. Folks wondered if this new baby was going to be as big as the storm that welcomed him. As it turned out, he was bigger!

He's bigger than all our other babies combined—he must weigh 44 pounds!

No wonder! Look—he was born with a hammer in his hand!

12 Tall Tale Mini-Books • Scholastic Professional Books

John Henry worked on a plantation with his family. He mostly picked cotton, but whenever there was hammering to be done, John did it. Often, while John Henry worked, he would hear trains whistle in the distance. And he would dream.

I'm going to take my hammer and be a steel driver for the railroad one day.

12 Tall Tale Mini-Books • Scholastic Professional Books

One evening, as John Henry was hammering down a few loose nails on the porch, a stranger named Little Bill stopped by. John's mother gave the man something to eat and asked him why he was traveling in their neck of the woods. Little Bill told them he was on his way to work for the railroad. When John Henry heard where Little Bill was headed, he nearly dropped his hammer! This was his chance to do what he'd been dreaming of all his life.

I've dreamed of being a steel driver on the railroad my whole life.

You can't go, John Henry!

We must let him go. John Henry is a steel-driving man.

The railroad boss pointed to some hammers and drills. John Henry found the heaviest hammer. When Little Bill had the drill in place, John Henry reached back and swung that hammer hard. When the sparks settled, you could hardly see the drill, it was so deep in the rock!

I told you, I'm a steel-driving man.

You're hired! How did you do that?

Little Bill took John Henry to West Virginia, where the Chesapeake & Ohio Railroad was cutting straight through a mountain to make the Big Bend Tunnel. John Henry and Little Bill went to the railroad boss to ask for work.

12 Tall Tale Mini-Books • Scholastic Professional Books

John Henry was the best steel driver in the whole country. Little Bill had to use buckets of ice water to cool John's hammers down. When other steel drivers were sick, tired, or hot, John Henry did their hammering as well as his own. Sometimes he even used two hammers!

12 Tall Tale Mini-Books • Scholastic Professional Books

For a long time, John Henry's best friends were his hammer and Little Bill. Then he met Polly Ann. When John Henry looked into Polly Ann's coal-black eyes, his heart pounded like a hammer. When Polly Ann smiled at John Henry, sparks lit the air around them.

The next day, folks came from all over to watch the contest between John Henry and the steam drill. Polly Ann sat right up front. She wore her best blue dress and the smile John Henry loved. She tried not to look as scared as she felt. The contest went back and forth all day. First the machine was winning. Then John Henry. Then the machine. John Henry sang to keep his rhythm.

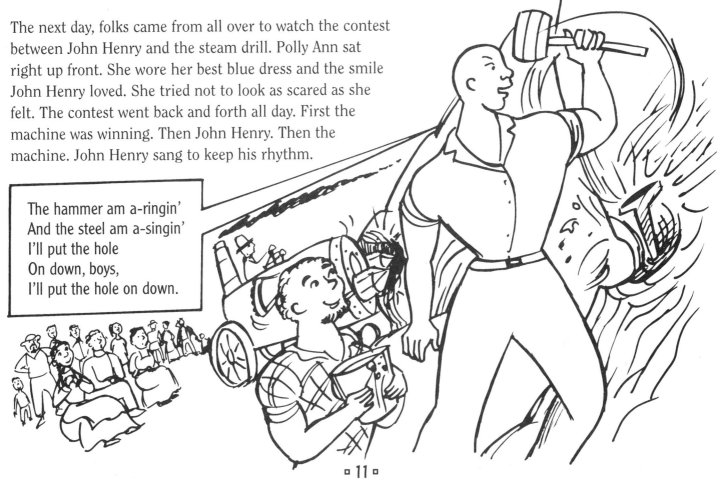

John Henry was very happy—he had work and a wife he loved. Then one day a city man came to the worksite. He was trying to sell a new invention, a steam drill, which he claimed could drill faster than a whole crew of men.

My John Henry can outdrill any machine ever built!

That's right!

If your man is faster than my machine, I'll give you the machine for free!

I ain't nothing but a steel-driving man. And I'll beat that steam drill, or die with a hammer in my hand.

Just before the sun set, the steam drill sputtered to a stop. John Henry gave one final swing with his hammer, then collapsed to the ground. While Polly Ann rushed to John Henry, the railroad boss and the city man measured the holes: John Henry's was 20 feet deep, the steam drill's was 19!

You won, John Henry! You beat that old steam drill!

My hammer, I need my hammer.

Little Bill handed John Henry his hammer. John Henry smiled one last time and died. Polly Ann, Little Bill, and the whole crew wept as the four strongest men carried John Henry's body to a hillside overlooking the train tracks. There they buried John Henry just as he'd lived and died: with a hammer in his hand.

Mose Humphreys

New York City in the mid-1800s was home to a group of lively young men called the Bowery Boys. The Boys had two jobs: fighting street gangs and fighting fires. Their leader in both was a big guy named Mose Humphreys.

Mose and his Boys spent part of each day fighting gangs like the Plug Uglies and the Dead Rabbits. When fists weren't enough to get the gangs to toe the line, Mose would hurl lampposts and paving stones at them.

Thank you for saving me, Mose.

Ain't I just doin' my duty?

After a muss, Mose usually headed over to his favorite soup house for a plate of pork and beans. He was a big man and had a big appetite.

The usual pork and beans, Mose?

Yeah. But make it a large piece of pork, and don't stop to count the beans.

Mose was 12 feet tall. He had hands as big as hams and feet as big as barges. He could swim the Hudson River in two strokes and circle the island of Manhattan in six. When he wanted to get from Manhattan to Brooklyn, he just jumped across the East River!

The only thing Mose loved better than fighting gangs was fighting fires. He belonged to Engine Company No. 40 and spent much of his free time polishing the *Lady Washington*, the fire company's shiny pumper engine.

I love this engine better than my dinner.

LADY WASHINGTON

12 Tall Tale Mini-Books • Scholastic Professional Books

Whenever the bell from City Hall tower sounded the fire alarm, all the volunteers rushed to the firehouse. Mose was always there first. After he put on his red shirt and hat, he would pull the pumper to the fire, while the other men rushed to catch up.

Come on, Boys! I can tell by the bells the fire's on Broadway.

Mose put out fires at mansions, tenements, soup houses, and churches. He rescued barbers, bankers, bakers, and babies. Mose especially loved to rescue babies.

Thank you so much!

Ain't I just doin' my duty?

The streets of New York were busy and crowded, and the road to the fire was not always clear. Sometimes a trolley blocked the way. Whenever that happened, Mose just set the fire engine down while he moved the trolley out of the way.

Don't drop us, Mose!

Have I dropped a trolley yet?

Mose's most famous rescue was of a baby trapped on the fourth floor of a burning tenement. When the baby's mother told the firefighters her baby was up on the fourth floor, the Boys got their longest ladder. But it reached only the third floor!

Man the pumps, Boys. I'll get her!

My baby! My baby!

Mose quickly piled three whiskey barrels one on top of the other. Then he put the ladder on top of the barrels. The ladder reached high enough, but it looked mighty shaky.

I'm going up!

That ladder's not steady! It will spill him!

Mose loved fighting gangs and fighting fires. He loved being needed. Then, one day, he found out he wasn't needed anymore. He and his Boys answered a fire alarm on the wharf. When they got there, a new horse-drawn steam engine was already putting out the fire.

Say good-bye to the old pumpers.

Your old pumper's no match for that machine!

When Mose saw how quickly the steam engine put out the fire, he knew the men were right. But he couldn't stand the thought of the *Lady Washington* sitting around collecting dust. So he picked up the old engine and, after giving her one last kiss, tossed her into the Hudson River.

The ladder swayed and the crowd gasped while Mose made his way to the fourth floor. He was just inside the window when the ladder caught fire. Everyone gasped. Then Mose reappeared, fire hat clutched to his chest, and leaped out of the window.

My baby! Where's my baby?

She's right here, ma'am. She's safe in my hat.

Three cheers for Mose!

12 Tall Tale Mini-Books • Scholastic Professional Books

Mose still fought street gangs, but he missed fighting fires. He missed having a big, fierce, dangerous enemy. Then he read a newspaper headline about bears attacking gold diggers in California. Bears and gold! California sounded like the place for Mose. So he moved to California and quickly found enough gold to fill his old fire hat and then some. Finding gold made Mose happy, but fighting bears made Mose even happier. The bears were big and fierce and dangerous, and all the prospectors were glad to have Mose around.

You are one brave man, Mose!

Ain't I just doin' my duty?

12 Tall Tale Mini-Books • Scholastic Professional Books

Joe Magarac

Imagine mining inside a mountain and discovering a giant man of steel buried beneath tons of iron ore! That's what one Pennsylvania miner did some 100 years ago: While mining for iron ore, he uncovered a steel giant named Joe Magarac!

One by one, the young steelworkers came forward to lift the first weight, a 350-pound bar. The audience cheered and Mary smiled when Pete Pussick lifted it easily over his head. Most of the others lifted it easily, too.

The next bar is heavier. Let's see how many of you can lift that!

500 lb.   850 lb.

Joe climbed out of the mountain and hopped a freight train to Pittsburgh. When he smelled stuffed cabbage, he jumped off the train and followed his nose to a picnic. At first no one noticed him; all eyes were on a platform where a man stood with his beautiful 18-year-old daughter.

Whoever does the best job lifting these steel bars will marry Mary this very afternoon.

I hope it's Pete Pussick.

350 lb.   500 lb.   850 lb.

□ 2 □

Each man came forward to try to lift the second bar. There were grunts and groans and enough sweat to make a small saltwater pond, but only three men managed to lift the 500-pound bar of steel. They were Pete Pussick, Eli Stanoski, and a big stranger from Johnstown.

Now we see men with a little muscle. Let's see who can lift the third bar, and marry my Mary.

Please let it be Pete.

850 lb.

□ 4 □

Pete tried to lift the bar, but nothing happened. Then Mary smiled at him and, in a burst of strength, he lifted the bar two and a half inches. Eli stepped up to the bar. Try as he might, he could only lift it an inch. All eyes turned to the Johnstown man. The big stranger bent and reached for the bar. He grunted and groaned but couldn't lift the bar off the ground. He looked at the audience, as if daring them to laugh. But nobody dared. Nobody, that is, except Joe Magarac.

Mary knew a deal was a deal so, although she was still crying, she walked over to Joe Magarac and offered him her hand.

Joe Magarac took several giant steps to the wooden platform. He lifted the 850-pound bar with one hand and the stranger from Johnstown with the other. The crowd gasped, Steve gulped, Pete frowned, and Mary burst into tears.

You're the strongest man here, but are you a steel man?

Of course I'm a steel man! Aren't I made of steel?

12 Tall Tale Mini-Books • Scholastic Professional Books

Everyone was happy. Mary married Pete, and Joe got a job at the local steel mill. He worked day and night at the number seven furnace. He left it only once a day to go to Mrs. Horkey's boardinghouse to eat.

Joe, don't you ever sleep?

No, ma'am. I work and I eat. That's all.

12 Tall Tale Mini-Books • Scholastic Professional Books

Joe was an amazing steelworker. The other men watched in awe as he stirred boiling metal with his bare hands, tasted hot steel for flavor, and squeezed warm steel between his fingers to make eight perfect steel rails at a time.

All of the steelworkers put their furnaces on a slow burn to keep them warm before heading home to their families. All except Joe Magarac, that is. Joe sat and stared into number seven furnace, dreaming of a bigger steel mill.

Three days later, the mill boss called the steelworkers back to the mill. The men were happy to be back to work. They wondered what Joe had done while the mill was closed. They went to number seven furnace to ask him, but he wasn't there.

Pete was right. Soon the mill yard was filled with rails. The
mill boss told the steelworkers that he had to close the mill
for a few days. The yard was too small to hold any more rails.

It's all Joe's fault!

Joe's a good guy, but
he works too hard.

We need a bigger mill
with a bigger yard.

12 Tall Tale Mini-Books • Scholastic Professional Books

Pete and the others followed the voice to a big bucket ladle filled
with boiling steel. In the center of the giant pot was the smiling
head of Joe Magarac.

You'd better get out
of there, Joe.

I think he wants to melt!

I want you to use my
steel to build the biggest
steel mill in America.

Before anyone could talk him out of it, Joe Magarac ducked
down and disappeared into the pool of molten steel. After his
bubbling laugh died away, the men poured the steel and
rolled it out. Soon Joe Magarac's wish came true: He became
the foundation of the biggest steel mill in America.

12 Tall Tale Mini-Books • Scholastic Professional Books

When Gib Morgan was 17 years old, the first oil well in the United States was drilled near his home in western Pennsylvania. That's a fact. As for the stories about Gib's life as an oilman, well, you can decide for yourself!

Back in the mid-1800s, when Gib was starting in the oil business, most men looked for oil using divining rods. They believed that if the forked sticks they carried turned in a certain direction, it meant they had found oil.

Of course, divining rods were a better indication of wind than oil, and Gib Morgan knew that. He had a better tool for finding oil—his nose! Gib prospected for oil by crawling across fields with his nose to the ground.

Gib Morgan was a complete oil gang all in one. This giant of a man prospected for himself. He built his own derrick. He did his own drilling. The only helper Gib Morgan needed was a personal cook, because all the work he did made him really hungry.

12 Tall Tale Mini-Books • Scholastic Professional Books

When Gib found oil, he quickly got to work bringing in the well. First, he dug a hole. Next he shot a bullet into the hole, to make it deep enough to drill. Then he sent his cable drill deeper and deeper until he hit oil. After that, he quickly built his derrick. Then he built oil tanks to catch the oil. Gib wouldn't stop to rest or to eat until oil was flowing into the tanks.

12 Tall Tale Mini-Books • Scholastic Professional Books

Even the few times his nose was wrong, Gib made the best of it. Once—it was before breakfast and Gib was very hungry—Gib's nose led him to drill. Gib brought in a well of pure buttermilk! That find kept Gib's cook busy for days.

I've been craving flapjacks. Looks like now I'll get some.

One icy cold winter, Gib brought in a gusher that froze as it sprouted out of the well. This might have been a problem for some men, but not for Gib Morgan.

You'll never be able to get that oil into a railroad tanker.

You're right! I'll cut it, then ship it east on flatbeds—which are a lot cheaper than tankers!

Gib knew there were lots of snakes in the jungles of South America. So he went in search of the longest snake he could find. He soon came across a sleeping snake that must have been a mile long. Gib picked it up and carried it back to where he was drilling.

Where did you find more cable around here?

It's not cable, it's a snake.

Gib tied the snake's tail to the end of the cable. Then he dropped the cable—and the snake—deeper and deeper into the earth. When the snake was about halfway uncoiled, Gib hit oil!

Great job! Thanks to you, we've hit oil!

Gib Morgan had drilled all over the United States when he got word that South America was practically floating in oil. Gib packed up some supplies, then he and his cook sailed to South America.

As soon as they landed, Gib began drilling. He dropped his cable lower and lower, but there was no sign of oil. Gib knew it was there, though, and he would keep drilling until he found it. The only problem was, his cable ran out before he hit oil.

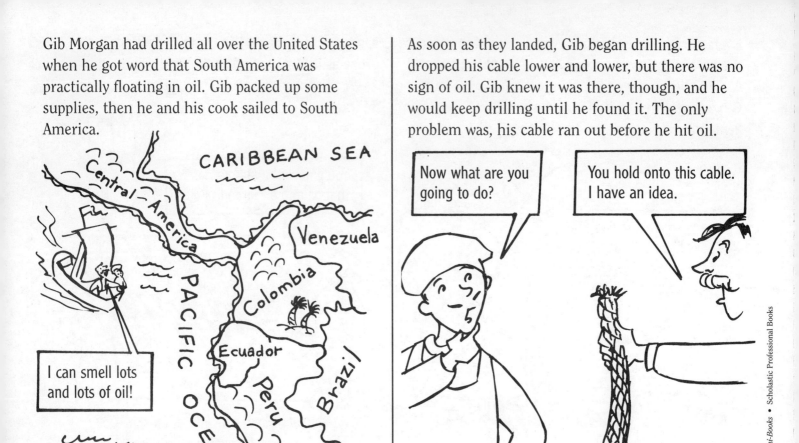

Gib returned to the United States richer than ever. So, when he smelled the world's biggest oil field right smack in the middle of Oklahoma, he gave the field to his friends. Well, they drilled and drilled and drilled, but found nothing. Finally, Gib had to take over. He went down one mile, two, three, four. Finally, when his drill hit the fifth mile, there was a deafening whoosh. Oil shot up to the sky and covered the entire state, making everyone happy—and rich.

Sam Patch

Sam Patch jumped over the Passaic Falls, Niagara Falls, and Genesee Falls the way most people jumped over a puddle. There was no mistake in Sam Patch—he always knew how to make a splash!

When Sam first started jumping, he didn't realize he was going to make a career out of it. He and the other boys who worked at the cotton mill in Pawtucket Falls, Rhode Island, jumped off the bridge into the Pawtucket River to cool off after a hard day's work.

I'll be the first one in—there's no mistake in Sam Patch!

Sam Patch showed an interest in jumping early on. As a baby, he jumped from his mother's arms into a basin of soapsuds. As a boy, his favorite game was leapfrog. When Sam got to school, he skipped over hard words when reading. At the time, his teacher thought he was lazy. When she read about him in the newspaper years later, she realized he had just been practicing jumping.

George Washington, father of our country, fought in the . . . War.

□ 2 □

Sam grew tired of jumping from the bridge. He looked around for something taller to jump from. His eyes fell on the mill. Sam decided to jump from the roof of the mill into the river. Spectators crowded the bridge to watch Sam jump. He did it— and came up smiling!

Hooray for Sam Patch!

I love to jump! There's no mistake in Sam Patch!

□ 4 □

After that, Sam Patch's jumping career took off. He leapt his way off bridges and cotton mills, into rivers, and onto headlines from Rhode Island to New Jersey.

In Paterson, New Jersey, a man by the name of Timothy B. Crane was building a bridge that would cross over the Passaic Falls. There was going to be a big celebration the day the bridge was pulled into place. Sam decided he would add to the festivities.

Just wait until the people see my bridge being pulled across the falls!

Just wait until they see me jump over the falls!

When the bridge had been pulled halfway across, the engineers lost hold of one of the guide ropes. It fell into the river below the falls. Sam knew this was his chance. He ran out from behind a tree, shouted, and jumped. He came up holding the guide rope!

Hooray for Sam Patch! He saved the day!

There's no mistake in Sam Patch!

The big day came. Mr. Crane worried that Sam Patch would take attention away from his new bridge, so he asked the police to keep Sam from jumping. Sam knew the police were looking for him, so he hid in the woods above the falls.

12 Tall Tale Mini-Books ▪ Scholastic Professional Books

Sam wondered if anything could top jumping into the Passaic Falls and helping to pull the bridge into place. He tried jumping off the bridge itself, but it just didn't give him the thrill he was looking for. He wanted something higher, something more exciting. Then he thought of it—he would jump Niagara Falls!

Sam built a jumping platform on Goat Island, a large rock in the middle of Niagara Falls. From the platform it was a straight drop of more than 100 feet into the swirling waters below. An audience of thousands watched in hushed silence as Sam climbed the platform.

12 Tall Tale Mini-Books ▪ Scholastic Professional Books

After a short speech, which was drowned out by the falls, Sam removed the handkerchief from around his neck and tied it around his waist. This was the signal that he was about to jump. Then he kissed the American flag and jumped off the platform. Sam hit the water. A moment later a sound that was even louder than the roar of the falls filled the air: It was the sound of applause as Sam shot out of the water, smiling!

The people waited and waited. After several hours, they slowly started to leave. They had different ideas about what happened to Sam Patch.

Some people might think a jump from Niagara Falls couldn't be beat, but not Sam Patch. Less than a month later, Sam decided to top his Niagara Falls jump with a 125-foot leap into the Genesee Falls in New York. Sam made posters announcing his jump.

On the day of the jump, Sam drew his greatest crowd ever. He made a short speech, which no one could hear, then moved his handkerchief from his neck to his waist. He kissed the flag, then jumped into the water. The people watched, and waited, for Sam Patch to reappear.

HIGHER YET!
Sam's Last Jump.
Some Things can be done as well as others

There's no Mistake in.

SAM PATCH.
—GENESEE FALLS—
Friday, Nov. 13, 1829, 2 o'clock

I'd better go see how that platform's coming along.

Where is he?

It's been a few minutes. You don't think . . . ?

He'll show up, just wait.

12 Tall Tale Mini-Books • Scholastic Professional Books

They were both wrong. Sam Patch jumped and survived, but the jump took him so deep that he popped up on the other side of the world. He settled in Australia and became a teacher. His students were kangaroos. Can you guess what he taught them how to do?

I'll make jumpers out of you yet. There's no mistake in Sam Patch!

12 Tall Tale Mini-Books • Scholastic Professional Books

Slue-Foot Sue and Pecos Bill

They say there's someone out there for everyone. That may or may not be true.
But it was certainly the case for Pecos Bill and Slue-Foot Sue.

Of course, Pecos Bill had never met Slue-Foot Sue. Sue was different from any other girl out West. Sure, she could kill a rattlesnake with her bare feet. But she could do it while she was shoeing a horse and singing a cowgirl song she wrote herself.

Bareback is how I love to ride.
I love to ride bareback during high tide.

Before he met Slue-Foot Sue, Pecos Bill was just a famous cowboy. He was so busy riding his horse Widow Maker, wrestling bears, branding cows, and inventing roping, he had no time to think about marrying. Besides, he'd never met anyone he wanted to marry.

12 Tall Tale Mini-Books • Scholastic Professional Books

When Pecos Bill first saw Slue-Foot Sue, she was doing what she liked best. She was riding a giant catfish in the Rio Grande. And she was riding it bareback!

That's the girl I aim to marry.

12 Tall Tale Mini-Books • Scholastic Professional Books

Bill waved and called to Sue. When Sue looked ashore, she nearly fell off her catfish. Bill was the biggest, boldest cowboy she'd ever seen. And Widow Maker was the handsomest horse. Sue steered her catfish to the riverbank. She slid off and nearly landed in Bill's arms. Neither one seemed to mind much.

It wasn't much more than a week before Bill asked Sue to marry him. The only reason she thought to say no was that she hadn't thought to ask first. But she figured that wasn't a good enough reason, so she said yes.

Bill fell so crazy in love he didn't know what to with himself. He was like a kid again, when he was raised by coyotes. He went to Sue's cabin every night, got down on all fours, and howled under her window. Luckily, Sue understood Coyote.

A-whoooo!
A-whoooo!

I love you, too, Bill.
I love you, too.

If you don't count bare feet and cowboy boots, Sue and Bill had a fancy wedding. Sue wore a beautiful white dress with a steel-spring bustle. Bill wore a new buckskin suit. Everyone wore smiles. As soon as the ceremony was over, Bill picked up Sue and gave her a big kiss. Their friends whistled and cheered for them.

What would you like for a wedding present? I'll give you anything you want.

Anything?

You see, ever since the day Sue first saw Bill and his horse, Sue had wanted to ride Widow Maker. But it had been such a whirlwind courtship, she had never had a chance to ask Bill if she could ride him. Now she had her chance.

Sue did not like to be told no. When Bill refused her request, she jumped out of his arms and stormed off toward the riverbank. Bill felt like she had a lasso around his heart and was taking it with her.

Sue bounced between the earth and the moon all day. Bill kept running and trying to catch her. Finally, he got a better idea. He took his lariat, which was as long as the equator, give or take a couple of inches, and whirled it above his head. He caught her and pulled her in.

When Sue heard Bill's words, she was back in a flash. Bill hardly had time to ask Widow Maker to go easy on his girl before Sue jumped on the horse. As soon as she did, Widow Maker bucked so hard he threw Sue as high as the new moon. Sue sailed over the moon and then started falling back down to earth. Bill ran to catch her. But before he got there, Sue hit the ground on her steel-spring bustle, and bounced straight back to the moon!

□ 10 □

After Sue's adventures in space, Texas seemed small to her. She and Bill took off to explore the world. The last anyone saw of them, they were riding giant crocodiles on the Amazon River.

□ 12 □

Alfred Bulltop Stormalong

When sailors put "A.B.S." after their names, it doesn't mean "Able-Bodied Seaman," as most people think. Sailors use the letters to honor the greatest sailor who ever lived—Alfred Bulltop Stormalong.

Stormy was a great sailor. He could scrub faster than 20 men, unfurl sails with his baby finger, and sing loud enough to scare away almost any hurricane. All the men on the *Lady of the Sea* loved him. All but the cook, that is.

That chowder was great. What's next?

Next? Did he ask what's next?

When he was 12, Alfred Bulltop Stormalong went to Boston Harbor to sign on as a cabin boy on the *Lady of the Sea*. Stormy chose the biggest clipper afloat because, at three fathoms—18 feet—high, he was a big boy, and he was still growing!

What's your name?

Alfred Bulltop Stormalong.

You look like an able-bodied seaman to me. You're hired!

12 Tall Tale Mini-Books • Scholastic Professional Books

Soon Stormy won over even the cook. After a morning of deep-sea fishing in the tropical Atlantic, the captain asked his crew to weigh anchor. They tried to lift the heavy metal hook, but nothing happened. Even Stormy couldn't budge it. They figured it must be a giant octopus! Stormy decided to take care of it. Stormy dove into the sea, which immediately erupted like a boiling cauldron. Then it grew quiet. The men felt sad, sure Stormy was dead. The boat tilted, and they prepared to meet their own watery graves. Then they saw Stormy climbing up the anchor chain.

What happened?

I tied every one of that octopus's arms in a different sailor's knot!

I'll never complain about feeding Stormy again!

12 Tall Tale Mini-Books • Scholastic Professional Books

Stormy loved the seafaring life. He would have stayed on the *Lady of the Sea* forever, except for one thing: He outgrew her. He was too big to sleep in a hammock like the other sailors; he had to sleep scrunched up in a lifeboat.

But Stormy kept his word. When the ship dropped anchor in Boston Harbor, Stormy said good-bye to his friends. He took one long, last look at the sea. Then, hoisting an oar over his shoulder, he headed west. He hoped the West was as big as he'd been told it was.

Stormy and the sailors began building the biggest clipper ship in the world. It took three years and caused a lumber shortage all over America, but the *Courser* was finally built. And what a ship she was! Her masts were so tall, they had to be hinged to let the sun and moon go by. Sailors climbed to the crow's nest as young men and returned with gray beards. And the deck was huge; the only way to get from bow to stern was on horseback—and even that took 24 hours!

When Stormy reached the great open spaces of Kansas, he settled down and became a potato farmer. That first year there was an awful drought. Stormy worked doubly hard, watering his crops with the sweat of his brow. He became the best farmer in Kansas.

Despite his success as a farmer, Stormy couldn't stop thinking about the sea. He missed the smell of the salt air, the sound of the surf, the feel of the ocean breeze. The sea was his home; he couldn't stay away any longer. He sold his farm and returned to Boston.

Look! It's Stormy!

But there isn't a ship here that's big enough for him.

We'll have to build it!

The *Courser* sailed the world over. The ship was too big to get into any harbor, but this wasn't a problem. The *Courser* was equipped with regular-sized ships for lifeboats, and these were used to ferry cargo to and from the mother ship.

Once, while sailing the English Channel between the French coast and the dark cliffs of Dover, it looked like the *Courser* might not make it. She was too big. Stormy had his men soap the sides of the boat. It worked! She slipped through the channel, barely rubbing the cliffs.

The hurricane then blew the *Courser* to the Gulf of Mexico and drove it straight toward the Isthmus of Panama. Stormy looked over the jungle and saw water on the other side. He put on more sail and plowed right through to the Pacific Ocean.

The *Courser* made history again in the Caribbean. It was hurricane season, which usually wasn't a problem, since hurricanes were like sunshowers to Stormy on his big ship. But an especially violent hurricane surprised him, blowing the *Courser* smack into an island.

12 Tall Tale Mini-Books • Scholastic Professional Books

After reaching the peaceful Pacific, Stormy decided to take the ship around the world one last time. He told his first mate that this would be his final voyage, that the *Courser* was getting too small for him.

The night before they reached Boston Harbor, Stormy died in his sleep. His shipmates doused his body with buckets of saltwater tears as they wrapped Stormy in hundreds of yards of Chinese silk. Then they buried him in the only place he ever felt at home, the sea, and said good-bye to their friend and hero Alfred Bulltop Stormalong, Able-Bodied Seaman.

12 Tall Tale Mini-Books • Scholastic Professional Books